THE CHINESE HOROSCOPES LIBRARY

DRAGON

KWOK MAN-HO

A DORLING KINDERSLEY BOOK

Senior Editor Sharon Lucas
Art Editor Camilla Fox
Managing Editor Krystyna Mayer
Managing Art Editor Derek Coombes
DTP Designer Doug Miller
Production Controller Antony Heller
US Editor Laaren Brown

Artworks: Danuta Mayer 4, 8, 11, 17, 27, 29, 31, 33, 35;
Giuliano Fornari 21; Studio Illibill 25; Jane Thomson; Sarah Ponder.

Special Photography by Steve Gorton. Thank you to The British Museum, Chinese Post Office,
The Powell-Cotton Museum, and The Board of Trustees of the Victoria & Albert Museum.

Additional Photography: Eric Crichton, Jo Foord, Steve Gorton, Dave King/The National
Motor Museum, Beaulieu, Stephen Oliver.

Picture Credits: The British Museum 15; Circa Photo Library 12; Percival David Foundation of
Chinese Art 19br; Courtesy of The Board of Trustees of the Victoria & Albert Museum 13.

First American Edition, 1994
4 6 8 10 9 7 5

Published in the United States by DK Publishing, Inc., 95 Madison Avenue,
New York, New York 10016

ISBN 1-56458-602-2
Library of Congress Catalog Number 93-48006

Reproduced by GRB Editrice, Verona, Italy
Printed and bound in Hong Kong by Imago

CONTENTS

INTRODUCING CHINESE HOROSCOPES

For thousands of years, the Chinese have used their astrology and religion to establish a harmony between people and the world around them.

The exact origins of the twelve animals of Chinese astrology – the Rat, Ox, Tiger, Rabbit, Dragon, Snake, Horse, Ram, Monkey, Rooster, Dog, and Pig – remain a mystery. Nevertheless, these animals are important in Chinese astrology. They are much more than general signposts to the year and to the possible good or bad times ahead for us all. The twelve animals of Chinese astrology are considered to be a reflection of the Universe itself.

YIN AND YANG

The many differences in our natures, moods, health, and fortunes reflect the wider changes within the Universe. The Chinese believe that

YIN AND YANG SYMBOL
White represents the female force of yin, and black represents the masculine force of yang.

every single thing in the Universe is held in balance by the dynamic, cosmic forces of yin and yang. Yin is feminine, watery, and cool; the force of the Moon and the rain. Yang is masculine, solid, and hot; the force of the Sun and the Earth. According to ancient Chinese belief, the concentrated essences of yin and yang became the four seasons, and the scattered essences of yin and yang became the myriad creatures that are found on Earth.

The twelve animals of Chinese astrology are all associated with either yin or yang. The forces of yin rise as Winter approaches. These forces decline with the warmth of Spring, when yang begins to assert itself. Even in the course of a normal day, yin and yang are at work, constantly changing and balancing. These forces also naturally rise and fall within us all.

Everyone has their own internal balance of yin and yang. This affects our tempers, ambitions, and health. We also respond to the changes of weather, to the environment, and to the people who surround us.

THE FIVE ELEMENTS

All that we can touch, taste, or see is divided into five basic types or elements – wood, fire, earth, gold, and water. Everything in the Universe can be linked to one of these elements.

For example, the element earth is linked to four animals – the Ox, Dragon, Ram, and Dog. This element is also linked to the color yellow, sweet-tasting food, and the emotion of desire. The activity of these various elements indicates the fortune that may befall us.

AN INDIVIDUAL DISCOVERY

Chinese astrology can help you balance your yin and yang. It can also tell you which element you are, and the colors, tastes, parts of the body, or emotions that are linked to your particular sign. Your fortune can be prophesied according to the year, month, day, and hour in which you were born. You can identify the type of people to whom you are attracted, and the career that will suit your character. You can understand your changes of mood, your reactions to other places and to other people. In essence, you can start to discover what makes you an individual.

DIVINATION STICKS
Another ancient and popular method of Chinese fortune-telling is using special divination sticks to obtain a specific reading from prediction books.

CASTING YOUR HOROSCOPE

*The Chinese calendar is based on the movement of the
Moon, unlike the calendar used in the Western world,
which is based on the movement of the Sun.*

Before you begin to cast your
Chinese horoscope, check your year
of birth on the chart on pages 44 to
45. Check particularly carefully if
you were born in the early months of
the year. The Chinese year does not
usually begin until January or
February, and you might belong to
the previous Chinese year. For
example, if you were born in 1961
you might assume that you were
born in the Year of the Ox.
However, if your birthday falls
before February 15 you belong to the
previous Chinese year, which is the
Year of the Rat.

THE SIXTY-YEAR CYCLE
The Chinese measure the passing of
time by cycles of sixty years. The
twelve astrological animals appear
five times during the sixty-year
cycle, and they appear in a slightly
different form every time. For
example, if you were born in 1952

you are a Dragon in the Rain, but if
you were born in 1976, you are a
Dragon Flying to Heaven.

MONTHS, DAYS, AND HOURS
The twelve lunar months of the
Chinese calendar do not correspond
exactly with the twelve Western
calendar months. This is because
Chinese months are lunar, whereas
Western months are solar. Chinese
months are normally twenty-nine to
thirty days long, and every three to
four years an extra month is added to
keep approximately in step with the
Western year.

One Chinese hour is equal to two
Western hours, and the twelve
Chinese hours correspond to the
twelve animal signs.

The year, month, day, and hour
of birth are the keys to Chinese
astrology. Once you know them,
you can start to unlock your personal
Chinese horoscope.

Water

Earth   **Gold**

Wood   **Yin**

Fire   **Yang**

CHINESE ASTROLOGICAL WHEEL
In the center of the wheel is the yin and yang symbol. It is surrounded by the Chinese astrological character linked to each animal. The band of color indicates your element, and the outer ring reveals whether you are yin or yang.

· DRAGON ·
MYTHS AND LEGENDS

The Jade Emperor, heaven's ruler, asked to see the Earth's twelve most interesting animals. When they arrived, he was impressed by the Dragon's power, and awarded it fifth place.

In China, the Dragon is the symbol of the Emperor, the son of Heaven, and represents male vigor. The blue-green dragon is associated with the east, sunrise, and the source of rain, and the white dragon is the ruler of the west and of death.

The Dragon is considered to be a good-natured creature and is believed to be blessed with magic powers. These powers include being able to shrink to the size of a silkworm; having the ability to swell up to fill the space between Heaven and Earth; and being able to choose to be invisible or visible.

There are four types of Dragon in Chinese mythology: heaven dragons symbolize Heaven's regenerative powers; spirit dragons cause rain; earth dragons rule springs and water; and there are dragons that guard

HONG KONG DRAGON
These striking 20th-century figures can be found in the Tiger Balm Garden in Hong Kong. The dragons represent yang, and they flank a phoenix, which represents yin.

EMPEROR'S ROBE
The color yellow and the five-clawed dragon show that this Ch'ing dynasty silk robe once belonged to a Chinese emperor.

treasure. There are also four dragon kings, believed to rule over the four seas that encircle the Earth.

THE SEA DRAGON
Once there lived a sea dragon king and his wife. One day the sea dragon's wife fell dangerously ill.

"The only cure for me is to eat a monkey's heart," said the wife. So the dragon rose to the sea's surface and floated toward the shore. He saw a big, fat monkey in a fruit tree that hung over the sea.

"Would you like to try the fruit in the trees on the other side of the sea? I could take you there," offered the dragon. "Thank you," replied the monkey, and climbed onto the dragon. As they dived beneath the waves, the dragon said, "My dying wife needs to eat a monkey's heart." "Oh dear," said the monkey, "I left my heart at the top of the tree. Let's go back and get it." The dragon rose to the surface of the sea. Once back on land, the monkey leaped off the dragon and ran up the tree. "Hurry and get your heart," cried the dragon. But the monkey just laughed and bounded off through the trees.

· DRAGON ·
PERSONALITY

The Dragon has a strong, energetic, and impressive character, and is never short of friends and admirers. It is usually found at the forefront of discussions or rallies.

One of the most charismatic animal signs in Chinese astrology, the Dragon is full of energy, power, and very good fortune. You have a vibrant, intelligent nature, and your actions are decisive and confident.

MOTIVATION
You are self-confident and curious, a combination that enables you to face challenges or difficulties with ease. Perfection is second nature to you, and you do everything to the best of your ability. However, you do not always allow other people to share the fruits of your labors. When you are

LACQUERWARE DRAGONS
Three dragons can be seen riding the waves on the lid of this 18th-century Chinese carved lacquer box.

disappointed, or when other people prove that they do not share your competence, skill, or forceful personality, you are usually very quick to show your frustration, impatience, and annoyance. This response is not the result of bad temper, but of your extreme sense of self-assurance, which makes it difficult for you to understand other people's weaknesses. In regard to financial affairs you are highly adaptable – you enjoy spending money, but when serious difficulties arise, you invariably manage to survive.

THE INNER DRAGON

Your vitality drives you to such an extent that you often race ahead without listening to the advice of others. Consequently, when you fail, it is difficult for you to recognize and accept your mistakes.

Although your sense of pride can sometimes verge on arrogance, other people tend to find you magnetically attractive. Despite your faults, you have a healthy and natural air, a warmhearted and frank approach, and a great love of the exciting and unpredictable that can make you seem thoroughly irresistible. As a friend you are exciting and generous, and as a parent you are encouraging and lively, although you can be very demanding. In your emotional relationships you are romantic and

charming, and possess great personal warmth. However, you value your freedom highly and tend to avoid serious commitments.

THE DRAGON CHILD

The young Dragon is intelligent, active, and needs its freedom. As a result, it is often difficult to control.

CLOISONNE JAR

This magnificent Chinese cloisonné jar depicts a yellow, five-clawed imperial dragon. It is from the period of the Ming dynasty, 1426–35.

· DRAGON ·
LOVE

The Dragon possesses great charm, energy, and charisma. It tends to treat love as a game to be played and enjoyed, but never to be taken too seriously.

When you are pursuing a new romance, your radiating confidence invariably leads to success. Perhaps it is your combination of enthusiasm and detachment that makes you so irresistible.

Although you have a passionate nature, love never takes over your life, and if all else fails, you are happy to be on your own. You make your partners feel lucky that you have chosen them. However, you recoil from overdependence and find emotional displays awkward and embarrassing.

Ideally, you are suited to relationships with the Monkey and the Rat. You share the Monkey's charm and enthusiasm, and never tire of its inquisitive nature. The Rat is likely to be besotted by you and its warmth and adoration should be a soothing influence.

Your encouraging nature should suit the Ram, but it may not flatter you sufficiently. The Snake's humor will temper your pride, but you may be stifled by its possessiveness. You share honesty and passion with the Tiger, but you

GODDESS OF LOVE
Kuan Yin is a powerful figure in Chinese mythology. Once a male Buddhist deity, she is now known as the goddess of mercy, and as Sung-tzu, the giver of children.

CHINESE COMPATIBILITY WHEEL

Find your animal sign, then look for the animals that share its background color – the Dragon has a pink background and is most compatible with the Monkey and the Rat. The symbol in the center of the wheel represents double happiness.

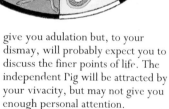

may have frequent arguments. Although you will find yourself attracted to other Dragons, you are both too authoritative for the relationship to last long. Your energy and drive may be too demanding for the patient Rabbit, but the independent Horse should find these traits endearing.

Romance with the Rooster or the Pig is likely to be troublesome. The Rooster will

ORCHID

In China, the orchid, or Lan Hua, is an emblem of love and beauty. It is also a fertility symbol and represents many offspring.

give you adulation but, to your dismay, will probably expect you to discuss the finer points of life. The independent Pig will be attracted by your vivacity, but may not give you enough personal attention.

Relationships with the Ox and the Dog could prove to be even more difficult. Although the Ox finds you invigorating, you will become restless in its company. The Dog could find you superficial, and it may need more tenderness than you could ever realistically offer.

· DRAGON ·
CAREER

The Dragon dislikes monotony and routine. It needs variety and stimulation, and is likely to experiment widely before it finds the career that suits it best.

False mustache and eyelashes

ACTOR
Life as a thespian is intriguing for the Dragon. It enjoys masking its true self in order to explore the individuality of someone else.

Actor's mask

ASTRONOMER
Gazing through a telescope to learn the secrets of the stars is very appealing to the Dragon. It excels in the careers that others might find unusual or difficult.

Astronomer's telescope

Porsche car

PRESIDENT AND CEO
In a large organization, the Dragon feels trapped and undervalued. It is much happier developing its own company, where its innovative approach can be used to best advantage.

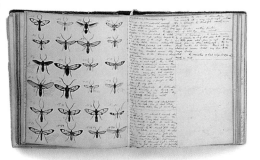

Naturalist's notebook

Butterflies

NATURALIST
The Dragon needs to feel free in its working environment. Open spaces and the natural world are a source of pleasure, and it can take great delight in recording its observations.

Chinese pen tray

ARTIST
This Chinese Ming dynasty pen tray might have been decorated by an artistic Dragon.

Lawyer's briefcase and documents

LAWYER
The professional relationship between client and attorney is often close. The Dragon thrives on this intimacy, but will not tolerate interference.

· DRAGON ·
HEALTH

Yin and yang are in a continual state of flux within the body. Good health is dependent upon the balance of yin and yang being constantly harmonious.

There is a natural minimum and maximum level of yin and yang in the human body. The body's energy is known as ch'i and is a yang force. The movement of ch'i in the human body is complemented by the movement of blood, which is a yin force. The very slightest displacement of the balance of yin or yang in the body can lead to sickness. Yang illness can be cured by yin treatment, and yin illness can be

cured by yang treatment. Everybody has their own individual balance of yin and yang. It is likely that a hot-tempered person will have strong yang forces, and that a peaceful person will have strong yin forces. When prescribing Chinese medicine, your moods have to be carefully taken into account. A balance of joy, anger, sadness, happiness, worry, pensiveness, and fear must always be maintained. This balance is known in China as the Harmony of the Seven Sentiments.

LINGCHIH FUNGUS
The fungus shown in this detail from a Ch'ing dynasty bowl is the "immortal" lingchih fungus, which symbolizes longevity.

TREE PEONY
When cooked in rice wine, tree peony bark can be taken in order to disperse bruises.

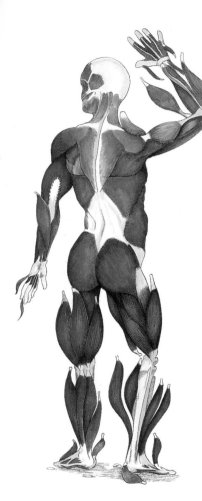

Born in the Year of the Dragon, you are associated with the element earth. This element is linked with the spleen, pancreas, stomach, muscles, and mouth. These are the parts of the human body that are most relevant to the pattern of your health. You are also associated with the emotion of desire and with sweet-tasting food.

The bark of the tree peony (*Paeonia suffruticosa*) is associated with your Chinese astrological sign. It is eaten in raw slices, with cinnamon and walnuts, to ease menstrual pains. When fried until dark and taken with safflower, it can control internal bleeding. It is also combined with chrysanthemum and honeysuckle to treat high blood pressure. Tree peony bark must never be taken during pregnancy.

Chinese medicine is highly specific; therefore, never take tree peony bark or any other natural medicine unless you are following advice from a fully qualified Chinese or Western doctor.

ASTROLOGY AND ANATOMY

Your element, earth, is linked with the digestive system. The stomach is a yang organ, and the pancreas, found behind the stomach, is a yin organ.

· DRAGON ·
LEISURE

The Dragon is stimulated by the thought of the unknown. It is always happy to try a new pastime or to embark upon an unexpected adventure.

SPIRITUAL QUESTS
It is often beneficial for the Dragon to embark on spiritual quests. It dreads confinement in any form and prefers to transcend its surroundings through action.

Incense and candle

Car tire, 1913

Bentley motor car

CAR RACING
Speed and open spaces are highly desirable to the Dragon. It would make an excellent race car driver and possesses good driving skills as well as a technical mind.

ENTERTAINING

Charisma is a useful quality for any entertainer to possess, and the Dragon has it in abundance. It loves to be the center of attention and will gladly entertain in its own home, using beautiful objects such as this 19th-century Chinese bowl.

Chinese bowl

ANTIQUES

The Dragon is an avid collector and likes to surround itself with interesting antiques such as this 19th-century wine cup and Ch'ing dynasty teapot.

Chinese wine cup

Chinese porcelain teapot

Espresso machine

Portuguese jug

TRAVEL

When the Dragon travels, it likes to experience the tastes, sights, and sounds of the local culture. It enjoys collecting objects during its travels, such as this Italian espresso machine and Portuguese jug, and making them part of its everyday life at home.

· DRAGON ·
SYMBOLISM

In Chinese astrology, each of the twelve animals is linked with a certain food, direction, color, emotion, association, and symbol.

Chinese cloisonné jar

COLOR
In China, fertile earth has a yellow hue. Yellow was the imperial color, worn by the emperor as the First Son of the Earth. The color yellow is also associated with the Dragon. This exquisite yellow and green jar is from the Chengte period of the Ming dynasty (1506–21).

FOOD
There are five tastes according to Chinese astrology – salty, acrid, bitter, sweet, and sour. Sweet foods, such as cashews, are associated with the Dragon.

Cashews

Antique
Chinese
compass

Section of a
map of Rome

DIRECTION

*The Chinese compass points south, whereas
the Western compass points north. The
Chinese compass has an extra direction,
the center, which is the Dragon's direction.*

ASSOCIATION

*The capital city and its life are
linked with the Dragon.*

SYMBOL

*The Dragon's symbol is the plumb line,
which is used to measure the depth of water.*

Plumb line

EMOTION

*Desire is the emotion that is
connected with the Dragon.*

Baby
expressing
desire

CHEERFUL DRAGON

~ 1904 1964 ~

This is a very happy Dragon. Since the Cheerful Dragon is associated with growth and fruitfulness, the very best aspects of the Dragon are emphasized.

You are linked to a beautiful bud about to burst into flower. This signifies that you have great potential, and it is most likely to come to fruition if you are gentle, kind, and helpful.

PERSONALITY
You are likely to be very physically attractive, and to have a strong sense of justice. You are very kind and compassionate, and do not use your talents solely for your own ends. When you encounter injustice, poverty, or cruelty, you can blaze out like a true Dragon.

YOUTH
Your youth may have been a difficult time. This is probably because you were full of unfulfilled potential, and this caused many problems. Perhaps you tended to be too impatient, and did not exercise enough self-restraint. Your strong feelings and powerful sense of right and wrong will probably drive you into the outside world with a vengeance, but do try to be patient.

Remember that to make the very best of your life, you should always try to give yourself sufficient time to learn, and develop, your strengths and skills.

FEMALE CHARACTERISTICS
Because of the calming and soothing influence of the yin force, the female Cheerful Dragon is always likely to be loving and strongly supportive to her partner.

CAREER AND FAMILY
Sometimes it may seem as if the Cheerful Dragon leads two separate lives. You tend to live a very open life at work and in your wider social circle, yet you are also an immensely

Cheerful Dragon

private person, and shelter your family from unwanted attention. It is probably necessary for you to develop this dual nature, because you often find yourself in the public domain, fighting fiercely for the issues in which you believe. The closed world of your private life can therefore act as an area into which you can retreat and gather further strength.

RELATIONSHIPS

When seeking a committed relationship, it is probably best for you to choose a partner who can offer you plenty of support.

PROSPECTS

After the initial difficulties of your youth, life is likely to treat you well. Luckily, success, prosperity, and material benefits should accrue to both you and your family.

Although you will invariably be involved in many different areas of life, none of these will seriously disturb you, unless you lose sight of the need for rest and recreation.

Look forward to what the future might bring. Your innate good fortune suggests that you should find yourself enjoying the finer things in life during your later years.

DRAGON FLYING TO HEAVEN

~ 1916 1976 ~

This Dragon is returning to the source of its power. The Dragon Flying to Heaven is in its natural environment and feels comfortable in most situations.

The Dragon Flying to Heaven is associated with the domestic hearth – the source of power, solace, and heat. Consequently you are a fortunate Dragon and can look forward to a very successful and enjoyable life.

PERSONALITY
Sometimes you may consider yourself superior to others. Try to blend your skills and fortune with compassion and humility. This should enhance your naturally well-balanced personality. As a result, you should enjoy your life to the fullest, and others should be able to enjoy their lives with you, too.

FRIENDSHIPS
Most Dragons tend to be popular and have many friends. You must try not to take people for granted, however. Just as the hearth is an area that can warm but also burn, so you need to take care with those around you. If you follow this advice, you are likely to enjoy real popularity and to gain the trust of your friends.

You tend to be very active, and this contributes to your success in life and also to your friendships. People enjoy your shining wit and your many skills. You have an alert mind, and this should help you to do very well in life.

You need to watch that you use your intelligence and your skills to the best ends, however. Always try to remember the dual nature of fire and the domestic hearth – both warmth and destruction.

Your vivacious personality and love of an active life are likely to bring you into contact with many people around the world. It is highly probable that you are particularly interested in learning from people

Dragon Flying to Heaven

who belong to different cultures. They, in return, are likely to consider you to be a good friend and a valuable confidant.

RELATIONSHIPS

You enjoy good fortune in the emotional side of your life. In a committed relationship, you share a sense of trust with your partner. In regard to family life, you should make a very good parent.

PROSPECTS

You should not be troubled by financial difficulties and are likely to live well. Try not to overspend, however. If you are sensible and enjoy your wealth but do not flaunt it, then you should never have to face disturbing financial problems.

Dragons usually fall on their feet – always be thankful for this good luck, and try not to despise those who do not share your natural good fortune.

YIELDING DRAGON

~ 1928 1988 ~

*Sometimes this Dragon seems a contradiction, for why
should a powerful creature have to yield? The answer lies in
your association with cutting instruments.*

Symbolically, your association with cutting instruments means that although you are a powerful Dragon, there is always a risk of your power being cut off, curtailed, or limited in some way.

PERSONALITY

You have a very complex nature, even for a Dragon. You are clever and popular. When you know what you want from your life, you go out and get it. At the same time, however, you recognize that you always need to be considerate, or even careful.

Although you are aware of your virtually unlimited potential, you sometimes fear that you might be unsuccessful if you overreach yourself. Unfortunately, this can happen, but your consideration and caution should eventually benefit you in this respect.

CAREER

At work, your superiors are likely to pay you considerable attention, and your career should invariably benefit as a result. Your skills and intellect should be highly appreciated, and you will be considered very versatile. By all means try to enjoy the good favor of your superiors, for you are likely to be offered many exciting opportunities for personal and professional advancement.

Be sure never to abuse this good favor. Always try to make the best of your opportunities, but keep a check on your innate Dragon arrogance, too. By keeping your confidence under firm control you should be successful without creating any negative feelings, or jealousy, in other people.

Always remember that other people may not be as fortunate as you. However, as long as you are

Yielding Dragon

thoughtful and considerate, you should continue to shine in various aspects of your life.

FRIENDSHIPS
Other people seem to be irresistibly drawn to you – they usually find you an attractive and exciting person to be with, and because of your natural kindness and thoughtfulness, you should manage to sustain your friendships and impress your acquaintances, too.

Beware of appearing overly "cocky" and proud, however, and try not to say anything that you will later regret. If you always try to balance your characteristic Dragon confidence with a certain humility and kindness, life should treat you very well indeed.

RELATIONSHIPS
You are likely to have a very good committed relationship with your partner, but may sometimes find it difficult to relate successfully to your children. Perhaps you need to allow them to enjoy the freedom of leading their own lives, rather than forcing them to always play the child's role in your family circle.

ANGRY DRAGON

~ 1940 2000 ~

As its name suggests, this is a volatile Dragon. Because of its powerful swings of mood, it is not an easy creature to be — nor to live with.

You are associated with two hands that are reaching out to grasp or to hold. Traditionally, this has often been interpreted as a struggle between two opposing forces. It is equally possible, however, to interpret the two hands as being supportive, for they could be holding something together.

PERSONALITY

You will have to learn to live with the possibility of inner tension. You have the choice of channeling the energies of two opposite poles into a supportive combination, or of being pulled apart by the conflict.

FEMALE CHARACTERISTICS

The female Angry Dragon is likely to have a strong, regimented approach to life. She may also tend to be very strict on the use, as well as the abuse, of money.

CAREER

All Dragons have a tendency to be arrogant and to give scant regard to other people's feelings or needs, and Angry Dragons in particular do not suffer fools gladly.

This innate ruthlessness can cause you to rise very swiftly to a position of considerable authority, but sometimes at great expense.

By always tending to put yourself first, you run the risk of spoiling or even destroying important personal relationships. Try to control this selfishness, for you might have to pay a very high price – your emotional relationships could eventually prove to be of even greater significance to you than any increase in material success and power.

However, your ruthlessness also gives you the strength to be very successful – in business, politics, and particularly in the military.

Angry Dragon

RELATIONSHIPS

Because of your powerful inner forces, you are likely to experience very stormy and dramatic relationships within your family, and especially with your partner.

As usual, the choice is yours. You can allow these unruly inner forces to rule you, accepting that they will probably make you react instinctively to your problems. Alternatively, you can try and harness these forces so they retain their strength but are directed in constructive and advantageous ways.

PROSPECTS

You have a real chance at greatness, wealth, and fame, but the cost in terms of human relationships might be very high. Try not to be drawn to the glitter of success unless you are absolutely sure that you can cope with the necessary personal sacrifice.

DRAGON IN THE RAIN

~ 1952 2012 ~

This is a hot, fiery, and active Dragon, which is in a cold and moist environment – the Dragon in the Rain is a perfect embodiment of yin and yang.

The influence of the yang force is responsible for the Dragon's arrogance and aggression. The Dragon in the Rain, however, is surrounded by the yin principle of coldness, moisture, and inactivity.

In classic Chinese paintings, the flying Dragon is usually depicted high among the rain clouds. It is a symbol of the yin and yang influences that always keep the world spinning.

You are associated with a man carrying a pole with loads on either side. Symbolically, this suggests that you have a balanced nature.

PERSONALITY
Your innate energies and arrogance tend to be contained. In the long run, this is for the best, but at first it may bring you trouble and strain. Your natural inclination is to be assertive and to assume that

everything will work out to your advantage, but this can be cramped by the yin influence. This means that you will probably always have to work very hard. Your yang drive meets your yin inaction, and no matter how hard you might fight against it, the yin force tends to slow everything down.

YOUTH
Unfortunately, you will probably have a difficult youth. You may often feel that you know where you ought to be going, but there always seems to be something that holds you back and restricts you.

Frustration is the inevitable result, but you must simply learn to live with it. Remember that ultimately, it will do you no good whatsoever to rebel against the yin influence that slows you down, for it is part of your personality.

Dragon in the Rain

RELATIONSHIPS

In emotional matters, if you can learn to hold your yin and yang in a constructive tension, then you will probably find that your committed relationship will happily mature. However, you must learn to be patient, and inevitably, there could be difficulties at first.

PROSPECTS

You certainly have the potential to enjoy a happy and prosperous future, but this is only likely to be possible if you manage to hold your yin and yang in creative tension. Once you

have achieved this inner balance, you should eventually succeed in various areas of your life.

Luckily, as you grow older, you are likely to find that your life becomes easier. You are linked to retirement, and this means that in your old age, you should manage to reap the benefits of holding your inner forces in balance.

Try not to be frustrated by the constraints that you will probably have to endure during your youth. It may be hard to believe at the time, but you are invariably storing up future benefits.

YOUR CHINESE MONTH OF BIRTH

Find the table with your year of birth, and see where your birthday falls. For example, if you were born on August 30, 1952, you were born in Chinese month 7.

1 You are hardworking, powerful, and successful, but may have difficulties with friendships.

2 You think clearly, listen to others, and enjoy challenges. Do not take risks with your money.

3 You are an excellent leader. You will do whatever is necessary to succeed in your course of action.

4 You are compassionate and determined. Your life may be hard, but you must learn to endure it.

5 You are intelligent, shy, and attractive. Your good friends will remain with you for life.

6 You are competitive, decisive, and can express yourself well. You should be highly successful.

7 Your life may be difficult initially, but should improve. Do not play with people's affections.

8 You are creative, but should be more critical, for the line between greatness and failure is very thin.

9 You are sensible, intelligent, and have good judgment. You are well balanced and should succeed.

10 You have many ideas and plans. Try to be more cautious, and learn to control your mood swings.

11 Your reticence can make some people feel uneasy. Learn to share more of yourself with others.

12 You are determined and a natural fighter. Try to balance these traits with consideration for others.

* Some Chinese years contain double months:

1928: Month 2	1952: Month 5
Feb 21 – March 21	May 24 – June 21
March 22 – April 19	June 22 – July 21

1976: Month 8
Aug 25 – Sept 23
Sept 24 – Oct 22

1904	
Feb 16 – March 16	1
March 17 – April 15	2
April 16 – May 14	3
May 15 – June 13	4
June 14 – July 12	5
July 13 – Aug 10	6
Aug 11 – Sept 9	7
Sept 10 – Oct 8	8
Oct 9 – Nov 6	9
Nov 7 – Dec 6	10
Dec 7 – Jan 5 1905	11
Jan 6 – Feb 3	12

1916	
Feb 3 – March 3	1
March 4 – April 2	2
April 3 – May 1	3
May 2 – May 31	4
June 1 – June 29	5
June 30 – July 29	6
July 30 – Aug 28	7
Aug 29 – Sept 26	8
Sept 27 – Oct 26	9
Oct 27 – Nov 24	10
Nov 25 – Dec 24	11
Dec 25 – Jan 22 1917	12

1928	
Jan 23 – Feb 20	1
* See double months box	2
April 20 – May 18	3
May 19 – June 17	4
June 18 – July 16	5
July 17 – Aug 14	6
Aug 15 – Sept 13	7
Sept 14 – Oct 12	8
Oct 13 – Nov 11	9
Nov 12 – Dec 11	10
Dec 12 – Jan 10 1929	11
Jan 11 – Feb 9	12

1940	
Feb 8 – March 8	1
March 9 – April 7	2
April 8 – May 6	3
May 7 – June 5	4
June 6 – July 4	5
July 5 – Aug 3	6
Aug 4 – Sept 1	7
Sept 2 – Sept 30	8
Oct 1 – Oct 30	9
Oct 31 – Nov 28	10
Nov 29 – Dec 28	11
Dec 29 – Jan 26 1941	12

1952	
Jan 27 – Feb 24	1
Feb 25 – March 25	2
March 26 – April 23	3
April 24 – May 23	4
* See double months box	5
July 22 – Aug 19	6
Aug 20 – Sept 18	7
Sept 19 – Oct 18	8
Oct 19 – Nov 16	9
Nov 17 – Dec 16	10
Dec 17 – Jan 14 1953	11
Jan 15 – Feb 13	12

1964	
Feb 13 – March 13	1
March 14 – April 11	2
April 12 – May 11	3
May 12 – June 9	4
June 10 – July 8	5
July 9 – Aug 7	6
Aug 8 – Sept 5	7
Sept 6 – Oct 5	8
Oct 6 – Nov 3	9
Nov 4 – Dec 3	10
Dec 4 – Jan 2 1965	11
Jan 3 – Feb 1	12

1976	
Jan 31 – Feb 31	1
March 1 – March 30	2
March 31 – April 28	3
April 29 – May 28	4
May 29 – June 26	5
June 27 – July 26	6
July 27 – Aug 24	7
* See double months box	8
Oct 23 – Nov 20	9
Nov 21 – Dec 20	10
Dec 21 – Jan 18 1977	11
Jan 19 – Feb 17	12

1988	
Feb 17 – March 17	1
March 18 – April 15	2
April 16 – May 15	3
May 16 – June 13	4
June 14 – July 13	5
July 14 – Aug 11	6
Aug 12 – Sept 10	7
Sept 11 – Oct 10	8
Oct 11 – Nov 8	9
Nov 9 – Dec 8	10
Dec 9 – Jan 7 1989	11
Jan 8 – Feb 5	12

2000	
Feb 5 – March 5	1
March 6 – April 4	2
April 5 – May 3	3
May 4 – June 1	4
June 2 – July 1	5
July 2 – July 30	6
July 31 – Aug 28	7
Aug 29 – Sept 27	8
Sept 28 – Oct 26	9
Oct 27 – Nov 25	10
Nov 26 – Dec 25	11
Dec 26 – Jan 24 2001	12

YOUR CHINESE
DAY OF BIRTH

Refer to the previous page to discover the beginning of your Chinese month of birth, then use the chart below to calculate your Chinese day of birth.

If you were born on May 5, 1904, your birthday is in the month starting on April 16. Find 16 on the chart below. Using 16 as the first day, count the days until you reach the date of your birthday. (Remember that not all months contain 31 days.) You were born on day 20 of the Chinese month.

If you were born in a Chinese double month, simply count the days from the first date of the month that contains your birthday.

1	2	3	4	5	6	7
8	9	10	11	12	13	14
15	16	17	18	19	20	21
22	23	24	25	26	27	28
29	30	31				

DAY 1, 10, 19, OR 28
You are trustworthy and set high standards, but tend to rush your projects. Try to be cautious, and do not be too self-obsessed. You may receive unexpected money but must control your spending. You are suited to a career in the public sector or the arts.

DAY 2, 11, 20, OR 29
You are honest and popular. You need peace, but also require lively company. You are prone to outbursts of temper. You tend to enjoy life and make the most of your opportunities. You are suited to a literary or artistic career.

DAY 3, 12, 21, OR 30
You are quick-witted, but may appear to be difficult. As a result, people may be wary of being your friend. You have a disciplined character and fight for the truth. You are suited to careers that have a competitive element.

Day 4, 13, 22, or 31

You are very warmhearted, but also have a reserved attitude, which can sometimes make you appear unapproachable. If you try to be more outgoing and sociable, you should become more popular. You have a calm and patient manner, and are suited to a career as an academic or researcher.

Day 5, 14, or 23

Your fiery, obstinate nature can sometimes make it difficult for you to accept suggestions or opinions from others, and your stubbornness may lead to quarrels or problems. You should be lucky with money and may often use your profits to set up new projects. Your innate intelligence will enable you to cope with a demanding career.

Day 6, 15, or 24

You have an open, stable, and cheerful character, and enjoy an active social life. You are affectionate and emotional, and have a tendency to daydream. This can lead to confusion, and your eagerness to help others may be stifled by your indecision. Although you will never be wealthy, you should always have enough money.

Day 7, 16, or 25

You enjoy a certain amount of excitement in your life, but must learn to become more realistic and disciplined. Although you are a natural performer, you should beware of alienating your friends or colleagues. In your career, the opportunity to travel is more important to you than a good salary or a high standard of living.

Day 8, 17, or 26

You have very good judgment, but should not act too quickly. Your social skills may sometimes be lacking, and you may alienate other people, so try to be more tactful. You will experience poverty, but also wealth. Your calm and determined nature is combined with a free spirit, making you best suited to self-employment.

Day 9, 18, or 27

You are happy, optimistic, and warmhearted. You keep yourself busy and are rarely troubled by trivialities. Occasionally you quarrel unnecessarily with your friends, and it is important for you to learn to control your moods. You are particularly suited to a career as a sole owner or proprietor.

YOUR CHINESE HOUR OF BIRTH

In Chinese time, one hour is equal to two Western hours. Each Chinese double hour is associated with one of the twelve astrological animals.

11 P.M. – 1 A.M. RAT HOUR
You are independent and have a hot temper. Try to think before you speak. Your thrifty nature will be useful in business and at home. You are willing to help those who are close to you, and they will return your support.

1 – 3 A.M. OX HOUR
Up to the age of twenty, your life could be difficult, but your fortunes are likely to improve after these troublesome years. In your career, be prepared to take a risk or to leave home during your youth to achieve your goals. You should enjoy a prosperous old age.

3 – 5 A.M. TIGER HOUR
You have a lively and creative nature, which may cause family arguments in your youth. Between the ages of twenty and forty you may have many problems. Luckily, your fortunes are likely to improve dramatically in your forties.

5 – 7 A.M. RABBIT HOUR
Your parents should be helpful, but your siblings may be your rivals. You may have to move away from home to achieve your full potential at work. Your committed relationship may take time to become settled, but you should get along much better with everyone after middle age.

7 – 9 A.M. DRAGON HOUR
You have a quick-witted, determined, and attractive nature. Your life will be busy, but you could sometimes be lonely. You should achieve a good standard of living. Try to curb your excessive self-confidence, for it could make working relationships difficult.

9 – 11 A.M. SNAKE HOUR

You have a talent for business and should find it easy to build your career and provide for your family. You have a very generous spirit and will gladly help your friends when they are in trouble. Unfortunately, family relationships are unlikely to run smoothly.

11 A.M. – 1 P.M. HORSE HOUR

You are active, clever, and obstinate. Try to listen to advice. You are fascinated with travel and with changing your life. Learn to control your extravagance, for it could lead to financial suffering.

1 – 3 P.M. RAM HOUR

Steady relationships with your family, friends, or partners are difficult, because you have an active nature. You are clever, but must not force your views on others. Your fortunes will be at their lowest in your middle age.

3 – 5 P.M. MONKEY HOUR

You earn and spend money easily. Your character is attractive, but frustrating, too. Sometimes your parents are not able to give you adequate moral support. Your committed relationship should be good, but do not brood over emotional problems for too long – if you do your career could suffer.

5 – 7 P.M. ROOSTER HOUR

In your teenage years you may have many arguments with your family. There could even be a family division, which should eventually be resolved. You are trustworthy, kind, and warmhearted, and never intend to hurt other people.

7 – 9 P.M. DOG HOUR

Your brave, capable, hard-working nature is ideally suited to self-employment, and the forecast for your career is excellent. Try to control your impatience and vanity. The quality of your life is far more important to you than the amount of money you have saved.

9 – 11 P.M. PIG HOUR

You are particularly skilled at manual work and always set yourself high standards. Although you are warmhearted, you do not like to surround yourself with too many friends. However, the people who are close to you have your complete trust. You can be easily upset by others, but are able to forgive and forget quickly.

YOUR FORTUNE IN
OTHER ANIMAL YEARS

*The Dragon's fortunes fluctuate during the twelve animal
years. It is best to concentrate on a year's positive aspects, and
to take care when faced with the seemingly negative.*

YEAR OF THE RAT
You are particularly
fortunate during this year
– it is likely to be an
excellent time for your financial
affairs and your professional life.
Make sure that you respond
positively and seize these good
opportunities as soon as they arrive.

YEAR OF THE OX
Although last year's
successes were very
enjoyable, unfortunately
they may have made other people
harbor jealous feelings toward you.
Try to be single-minded, and do not
allow their negative feelings to
distract you unnecessarily.

YEAR OF THE TIGER
This can be a successful
year, but only if you are
willing to make serious

changes in your life. It is likely that
you will move away from your home
environment, and perhaps even to
another country.

YEAR OF THE RABBIT
Unfortunately, you are
likely to suffer from
various illnesses this year.
You may feel that traveling will be
an effective form of escape and
stimulation, but travel in the Year of
the Rabbit will only exacerbate your
ill health further.

YEAR OF THE DRAGON
Your tremendous drive
and personal skills will
create many opportunities
this year, which should stretch you
to your utmost. Channel your energy
into these opportunities by all
means, but do not forget to apply
yourself to study.

YEAR OF THE SNAKE
Everything that you decide to try your hand at this year should prove to be a great success, for the Year of the Snake is an excellent year for the Dragon. However, this year you must be particularly careful to pay proper respects to the dead.

YEAR OF THE HORSE
This is likely to be a year of considerable difficulty and hardship, and there could be a death in your family. These negative elements will combine in the Year of the Horse to make you feel unsettled in various areas of your life.

YEAR OF THE RAM
You will seem to be pursued by accidents, quarrels, and controversy throughout the Year of the Ram. Do not despair, however. If you take care of yourself and act with sense and caution, everything will eventually be satisfactorily resolved.

YEAR OF THE MONKEY
This year is a time of considerable trouble and disruption in your family life, professional life, and social life. Unfortunately, there is little respite in the Year of the Monkey, and even your relationship with your parents could suffer.

YEAR OF THE ROOSTER
Although you are likely to find yourself suffering from minor ailments, you should still be able to enjoy good fortune this year. Make every effort to enjoy the potential for success in the various areas of your life.

YEAR OF THE DOG
Difficulties pursue you during the Year of the Dog, and nothing whatsoever seems to go smoothly for you. There is no point in getting upset by your fortune this year — develop your patience, and hope for better times in the future.

YEAR OF THE PIG
You are likely to enjoy excellent fortune in the Year of the Pig, for it is a very auspicious year for the Dragon. Everything should work out to your advantage, and you should enjoy particular success in your emotional affairs.

YOUR CHINESE
YEAR OF BIRTH

*Your astrological animal corresponds to the Chinese year of
your birth. It is the single most important key in the quest
to unlock your Chinese horoscope.*

Find your Western year of birth in
the left-hand column of the chart.
Your Chinese astrological animal is
on the same line as your year of birth
in the right-hand column of the
chart. If you were born in the
beginning of the year, check the

middle column of the chart carefully.
For example, if you were born in
1965, you might assume that you
belong to the Year of the Snake.
However, if your birthday falls
before February 2, you actually
belong to the Year of the Dragon.

1900	Jan 31 – Feb 18, 1901	Rat
1901	Feb 19 – Feb 7, 1902	Ox
1902	Feb 8 – Jan 28, 1903	Tiger
1903	Jan 29 – Feb 15, 1904	Rabbit
1904	Feb 16 – Feb 3, 1905	Dragon
1905	Feb 4 – Jan 24, 1906	Snake
1906	Jan 25 – Feb 12, 1907	Horse
1907	Feb 13 – Feb 1, 1908	Ram
1908	Feb 2 – Jan 21, 1909	Monkey
1909	Jan 22 – Feb 9, 1910	Rooster
1910	Feb 10 – Jan 29, 1911	Dog
1911	Jan 30 – Feb 17, 1912	Pig
1912	Feb 18 – Feb 5, 1913	Rat
1913	Feb 6 – Jan 25, 1914	Ox
1914	Jan 26 – Feb 13, 1915	Tiger
1915	Feb 14 – Feb 2, 1916	Rabbit
1916	Feb 3 – Jan 22, 1917	Dragon

1917	Jan 23 – Feb 10, 1918	Snake
1918	Feb 11 – Jan 31, 1919	Horse
1919	Feb 1 – Feb 19, 1920	Ram
1920	Feb 20 – Feb 7, 1921	Monkey
1921	Feb 8 – Jan 27, 1922	Rooster
1922	Jan 28 – Feb 15, 1923	Dog
1923	Feb 16 – Feb 4, 1924	Pig
1924	Feb 5 – Jan 23, 1925	Rat
1925	Jan 24 – Feb 12, 1926	Ox
1926	Feb 13 – Feb 1, 1927	Tiger
1927	Feb 2 – Jan 22, 1928	Rabbit
1928	Jan 23 – Feb 9, 1929	Dragon
1929	Feb 10 – Jan 29, 1930	Snake
1930	Jan 30 – Feb 16, 1931	Horse
1931	Feb 17 – Feb 5, 1932	Ram
1932	Feb 6 – Jan 25, 1933	Monkey
1933	Jan 26 – Feb 13, 1934	Rooster

1934	Feb 14 – Feb 3, 1935	Dog	1971	Jan 27 – Feb 14, 1972	Pig
1935	Feb 4 – Jan 23, 1936	Pig	1972	Feb 15 – Feb 2, 1973	Rat
1936	Jan 24 – Feb 10, 1937	Rat	1973	Feb 3 – Jan 22, 1974	Ox
1937	Feb 11 – Jan 30, 1938	Ox	1974	Jan 23 – Feb 10, 1975	Tiger
1938	Jan 31 – Feb 18, 1939	Tiger	1975	Feb 11 – Jan 30, 1976	Rabbit
1939	Feb 19 – Feb 7, 1940	Rabbit	1976	Jan 31 – Feb 17, 1977	Dragon
1940	Feb 8 – Jan 26, 1941	Dragon	1977	Feb 18 – Feb 6, 1978	Snake
1941	Jan 27 – Feb 14, 1942	Snake	1978	Feb 7 – Jan 27, 1979	Horse
1942	Feb 15 – Feb 4, 1943	Horse	1979	Jan 28 – Feb 15, 1980	Ram
1943	Feb 5 – Jan 24, 1944	Ram	1980	Feb 16 – Feb 4, 1981	Monkey
1944	Jan 25 – Feb 12, 1945	Monkey	1981	Feb 5 – Jan 24, 1982	Rooster
1945	Feb 13 – Feb 1, 1946	Rooster	1982	Jan 25 – Feb 12, 1983	Dog
1946	Feb 2 – Jan 21, 1947	Dog	1983	Feb 13 – Feb 1, 1984	Pig
1947	Jan 22 – Feb 9, 1948	Pig	1984	Feb 2 – Feb 19, 1985	Rat
1948	Feb 10 – Jan 28, 1949	Rat	1985	Feb 20 – Feb 8, 1986	Ox
1949	Jan 29 – Feb 16, 1950	Ox	1986	Feb 9 – Jan 28, 1987	Tiger
1950	Feb 17 – Feb 5, 1951	Tiger	1987	Jan 29 – Feb 16, 1988	Rabbit
1951	Feb 6 – Jan 26, 1952	Rabbit	1988	Feb 17 – Feb 5, 1989	Dragon
1952	Jan 27 – Feb 13, 1953	Dragon	1989	Feb 6 – Jan 26, 1990	Snake
1953	Feb 14 – Feb 2, 1954	Snake	1990	Jan 27 – Feb 14, 1991	Horse
1954	Feb 3 – Jan 23, 1955	Horse	1991	Feb 15 – Feb 3, 1992	Ram
1955	Jan 24 – Feb 11, 1956	Ram	1992	Feb 4 – Jan 22, 1993	Monkey
1956	Feb 12 – Jan 30, 1957	Monkey	1993	Jan 23 – Feb 9, 1994	Rooster
1957	Jan 31 – Feb 17, 1958	Rooster	1994	Feb 10 – Jan 30, 1995	Dog
1958	Feb 18 – Feb 7, 1959	Dog	1995	Jan 31 – Feb 18, 1996	Pig
1959	Feb 8 – Jan 27, 1960	Pig	1996	Feb 19 – Feb 6, 1997	Rat
1960	Jan 28 – Feb 14, 1961	Rat	1997	Feb 7 – Jan 27, 1998	Ox
1961	Feb 15 – Feb 4, 1962	Ox	1998	Jan 28 – Feb 15, 1999	Tiger
1962	Feb 5 – Jan 24, 1963	Tiger	1999	Feb 16 – Feb 4, 2000	Rabbit
1963	Jan 25 – Feb 12, 1964	Rabbit	2000	Feb 5 – Jan 23, 2001	Dragon
1964	Feb 13 – Feb 1, 1965	Dragon	2001	Jan 24 – Feb 11, 2002	Snake
1965	Feb 2 – Jan 20, 1966	Snake	2002	Feb 12 – Jan 31, 2003	Horse
1966	Jan 21 – Feb 8, 1967	Horse	2003	Feb 1 – Jan 21, 2004	Ram
1967	Feb 9 – Jan 29, 1968	Ram	2004	Jan 22 – Feb 8, 2005	Monkey
1968	Jan 30 – Feb 16, 1969	Monkey	2005	Feb 9 – Jan 28, 2006	Rooster
1969	Feb 17 – Feb 5, 1970	Rooster	2006	Jan 29 – Feb 17, 2007	Dog
1970	Feb 6 – Jan 26, 1971	Dog	2007	Feb 18 – Feb 6, 2008	Pig